DATE DUE

		8/8/ffo ✓
		8/5/10 ✓
		8/d/10 ✓
		8/5d/10 ✓
		8/d8/10 ✓
		8/d80 ✓

The Earth's Weather

Rebecca Harman

Heinemann Library
Chicago, Illinois

© Heinemann Library 2005
a division of Reed Elsevier Inc.
Chicago, Illinois

Customer Service 888-454-2279
Visit our website at www.heinemannlibrary.com

Editorial: Melanie Copland
Design: Victoria Bevan and AMR Design
Illustration: Art Construction and
David Woodroffe
Picture Research: Mica Brancic and Helen Reilly
Production: Duncan Gilbert

Originated by Chroma Graphics (Overseas) Pte. Ltd
Printed in China by WKT Company Limited

09 08 07 06 05
10 9 8 7 6 5 4 3 2 1

Library of Congress Cataloging-in-Publication Data

Harman, Rebecca.
  The Earth's weather / Rebecca Harman.
    p. cm. -- (Earth's processes)
  Includes bibliographical references and index.
  ISBN 1-4034-7058-8 (lib. bdg.) -- ISBN 1-4034-7065-0 (pbk.)
  1. Weather--Juvenile literature. 2. Meteorology--Juvenile literature. I. Title. II. Series.
  QC981.3.H365 2005
  551.6--dc22

                                                              2005010645

Acknowledgments
The Publishers would like to thank the following for permission to reproduce photographs:
Corbis, **p.28**; Press Association/Eric Gay **p.19**; Press Association/LM Otero **p.21**; Press Association
p.23; Press Association/Diario la Republica **p.25**; Press Association/Yesikka Vivancos **p.26**; Science
Photo Library/NASA **p.10**; Science Photo Library/Alex Maclean **pp.17, 18**; Science Photo Library
p.27; SPL **p.7**; Still Pictures/Weatherstock **p.4**; Still Pictures/Qinetiq LTD **p.5**; Still Pictures/Jim Wark **p.6**;
Still Pictures/Philippe Hays **p.11**; Still Pictures/Ted Mead/WWI **p.12**; Still Pictures/Carlo Dani & Ingrid
Jeske **p.16**; Science Photo Library **p.20**; Still Pictures/Weatherstock, **p.22**.

Cover photograph of lightning reproduced with permission from Corbis.

The Publishers would like to thank Nick Lapthorn for his assistance in the preparation of this book.

Every effort has been made to contact copyright holders of any material reproduced in this
book. Any omissions will be rectified in subsequent printings if notice is given to the publisher.

Contents

Words appearing in the text in bold, like this, are explained in the Glossary.

What is Weather?

Have you ever been woken up during the night by thunder and lightning? You might have gotten up and watched the lightning strikes through the window. You might have counted the seconds in between seeing the lightning flash and hearing the thunder to work out how distant the storm is. A **thunderstorm** is just one example of a **weather** event.

The weather is what happens in the **atmosphere** in one place at one point in time. The atmosphere is a blanket of air that surrounds Earth and is held down by **gravity**. All weather takes place in the atmosphere. Weather can be a snowstorm in New York City, a sunny sky above San Diego, California, or a **hurricane** off the coast of Florida.

Being caught outside in a thunderstorm can be a very frightening experience.

Is weather the same as climate?

Weather should not be confused with **climate**. The climate of an area is the total of all the day-to-day weather in that location over about 30 years. So climate is the general weather an area is likely to experience. For example, if an area has a lot of rain, then we say it has a wet climate, even though it may not rain every day. This is different from describing the weather of the area. Weather can change every day, and sometimes many times in one day!

A satellite image is a photograph taken from space. In this image you can see that the atmosphere forms a blanket of air around Earth.

All the information you need to find out about the weather is outside. Go outside and look up at the sky. You might see the Sun, you might see clouds, or you might see rain, hail, or snow. Cold air and wind could blow in your face. This is all weather, and next time you look, it may be different.

Did you know?

The weather is always changing, in some areas very quickly and sometimes violently. A damaging hailstorm can last just five minutes.

All weather takes place in the atmosphere.

What are the ingredients of weather?

There are three main ingredients in weather. These are **air pressure**, **temperature**, and **humidity**. In the same way that you mix ingredients together to make a cake, these weather ingredients get mixed together in the atmosphere to form different types of weather.

Did you know?

Scientists who study the weather are called **meteorologists**. In much the same way that a doctor examines patients to determine their condition, meteorologists look at the condition of the atmosphere to **predict** what will happen next. Most weather presenters on television are meteorologists. They do not just tell us about the weather, they study it as well, and try to predict what it will do.

These meteorologists are preparing to launch a weather balloon into a tornado in Kansas.

What is air pressure?

As the atmosphere rests on Earth's surface it pushes down on it. This is air pressure. Cold air is heavier than warm air, so cold air has a higher pressure. Air pressure is measured using an instrument called a **barometer**. Differences in pressure from one area to another produce winds. Winds blow from high to low pressure.

A thermometer measures how hot or cold the air is. In the Fahrenheit scale, water freezes at 32 °F and boils at 212 °F. In the Celsius scale, water freezes at 0 °C and boils at 100 °C.

What is temperature?

The temperature of a place is how hot or cold it is. This is measured using an instrument called a **thermometer**. A thermometer records the temperature in degrees Fahrenheit (°F)and degrees Celsius (°C). Differences in temperature cause differences in pressure. If air becomes warmer, it will rise, resulting in lower pressure. If air becomes colder, it will sink, resulting in higher pressure.

What is humidity?

Humidity is the amount of moisture in the air. The moisture is an invisible gas called **water vapor**. If humidity is high, there is a good chance of **precipitation** (rain, sleet, snow, or hail). The humidity depends on the temperature of the air, as colder air can hold less moisture than warmer air.

C	F	
100	212	◄ boiling point of water
90	194	
80	176	
70	158	
60	140	136°F (58°C) highest temperature recorded ◄ in the world, Libya, September 1922
50	122	
40	104	◄ a very hot day
30	86	
20	68	
10	50	
0	32	◄ freezing point of water
−10	14	
−20	−4	
−30	−22	◄ a very cold day
−40	−40	
−50	−58	
−60	−76	
−70	−94	
−80	−112	-127°F (-88°C) lowest temperature recorded in ◄ the world, Antarctica, August 1960
−50	−130	
−80	−148	
C	F	

What Creates Earth's Weather?

During the day the Sun shines on Earth, warming the surface and the atmosphere above it. The Sun does not, however, shine evenly on Earth's surface.

At the **Equator** it is warm throughout the year. The Sun is almost directly overhead, so heat is concentrated in a small area. This is why it is so hot in countries close to the Equator.

Farther north or south of the Equator, the Sun is not directly overhead. It is at an angle in the sky, so the heat is spread over a larger area. This means the surface and atmosphere receive less heat, so it is cooler than at the Equator.

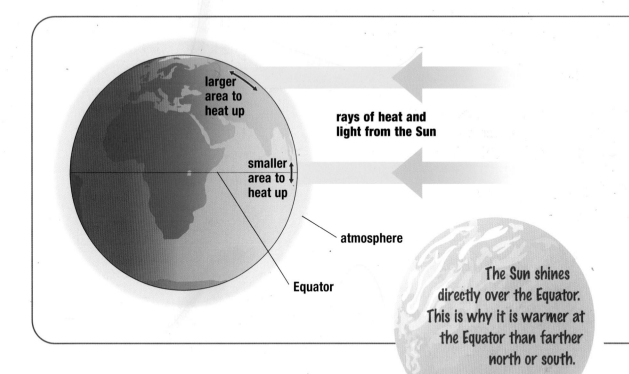

larger area to heat up

rays of heat and light from the Sun

smaller area to heat up

atmosphere

Equator

The Sun shines directly over the Equator. This is why it is warmer at the Equator than farther north or south.

Did you know?

The Sun is 93 million miles (150 million kilometers) from Earth. It provides the **energy** to create Earth's weather. This energy is in the form of light and heat.

The weather is the result of this uneven heating of Earth's surface. Heat always moves from where it is hot to where it is cold. Warm air from the Equator moves toward colder parts of the world and heats them up. The warm air is blown by winds to the colder areas north and south of the Equator.

Winds do not just move air across Earth. They also move air up and down in the atmosphere. When the air close to the ground at the Equator is heated, it becomes lighter than the air above it, so it rises. As the warm air rises, colder, heavier air sinks to take its place.

As a result of all this, air at the Equator is heated, rises up and moves to the north or south. The space left is filled by cold air that is blown toward the Equator. This cold air is then heated, and the cycle begins again. This cycle of moving air creates all the weather we see on Earth.

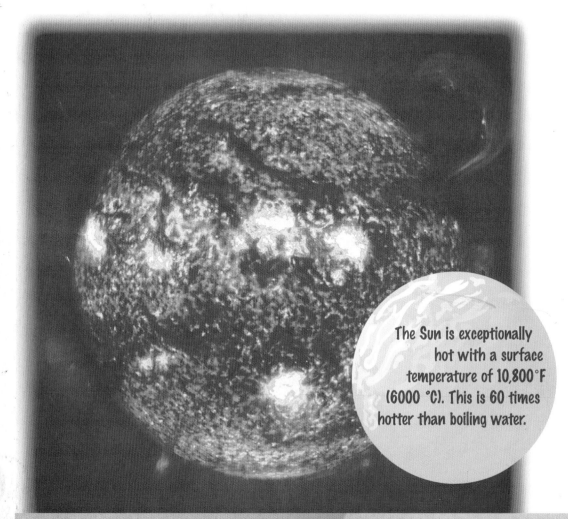

The Sun is exceptionally hot with a surface temperature of 10,800 °F (6000 °C). This is 60 times hotter than boiling water.

Why Does the Weather Change?

Changes in the weather are caused by changes in the pressure, temperature, and humidity of the air. This happens as the air moves from warm to cold areas and from cold areas to warm ones.

This movement of air produces two main pressure systems:

- areas of low pressure, called **lows**
- areas of high pressure, called **highs**

Each has very different types of weather.

Low pressure systems are also called **depressions**. These are areas of the atmosphere where pressure is lower than in the surrounding areas because air is rising. As the air rises it cools. Cold air cannot carry as much moisture as warm air, so some of the water vapor in the air **condenses**. It changes into tiny drops of water and produces clouds and rain.

In England, London often has bad weather as a result of low pressure systems.

Did you know?

Low pressure systems can be huge. Just one low may cover the entire Midwest.

High pressure systems are also called **anticyclones**. These are areas of the atmosphere where pressure is higher than in the surrounding areas because air is falling. This has the opposite effect to a low. As the air falls, it is warmed. This produces sunny, dry weather.

Highs and lows are continually forming, moving across Earth and dying away. Lows usually last for only a few days. In Great Britain and Ireland, the weather can change very quickly because of lows blowing in from across the Atlantic Ocean. This means that one summer day may be dry, warm, and calm, while the next day may be wet, cool, and windy. Highs sometimes last a lot longer. When this happens they are called blocking anticyclones, because they force all other weather to travel around them. The Sahara Desert is one example of a place that has high pressure and sunny skies for most of the year.

A high pressure system brings clear skies. The Sun will heat the ground up quickly during the day, but at night it will be cold because there are no clouds to keep the heat from escaping.

What is an Air Mass?

An air mass is a very large area of air with similar pressure, temperature, and humidity. An air mass can be so big that it can cover half of the United States.

An air mass forms when air stays still for a long period of time (a few weeks to a few months) over one area. This area is called the source region. The air mass takes on the same pressure, temperature, and humidity as its source region. Air over the Arctic Ocean, for example, will become cold and wet, while air over the Sahara Desert will become warm and dry.

Air masses drift slowly away from their source regions for thousands of miles. As an air mass moves, it keeps the same pressure, temperature, and humidity, because it does not mix with other air masses. This means it will change the weather in the areas it moves over. For example, if an air mass formed over northern Canada moves south over the United States, it will bring cold, dry weather with it.

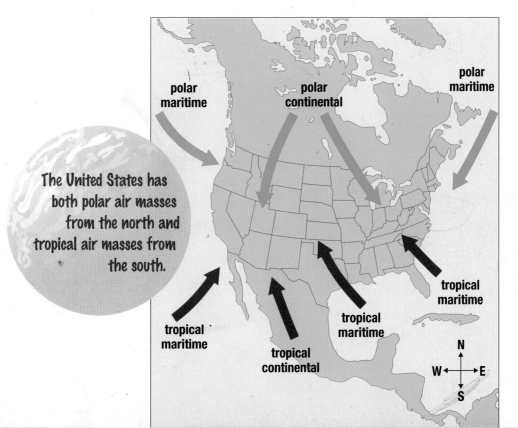

The United States has both polar air masses from the north and tropical air masses from the south.

13

Did you know?

There are four main types of air mass, depending on their source region:

- Polar continental—this type of air mass forms over land in **polar regions**. These are very cold ice and snow covered regions, such as northern Canada and Alaska. It produces very cold, dry weather in winter and cool, pleasant weather in summer.

- Polar maritime—this type of air mass forms over oceans in polar regions, such as the Arctic Ocean. It produces cool, wet weather in the areas it travels over.

- Tropical continental—this type of air mass forms over land in **tropical regions**. These are very hot areas, such as northern Mexico and the Sahara Desert. It produces hot, dry weather with clear skies.

- Tropical maritime—this type of air mass forms over oceans near the **Equator**, such as the eastern Pacific Ocean and the Caribbean Sea. It produces warm, wet weather.

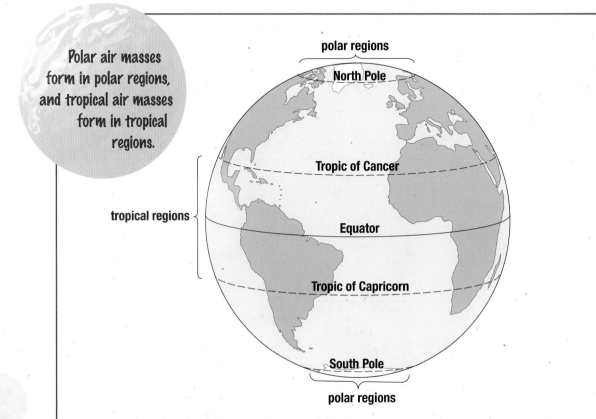

Polar air masses form in polar regions, and tropical air masses form in tropical regions.

polar regions

North Pole

Tropic of Cancer

tropical regions

Equator

Tropic of Capricorn

South Pole

polar regions

What is a Weather Front?

Air masses do not mix with other air masses. This means that a boundary forms between air masses when they meet. This boundary is called a **front**. At a front, one air mass tries to move the other out of the way so that it can continue its journey.

As polar air masses move toward the Equator, and tropical air masses move toward the poles, they usually meet over North America, the North Atlantic, and Europe. When they bump into each other this results in an exciting display of weather activity. This is why the weather is so changeable in these areas.

When a tropical air mass with its warmer, lighter air moves towards a polar air mass with its colder, heavier air, the warm air rises up over the cold air. This is because the warm air is lighter than cold air. As the warm air rises, it cools and condenses to produce clouds and rain. The place where this happens is called a **warm front**.

At the warm front, warm air rises up above cold air producing a wide band of clouds and rain. At the cold front, cold air cuts under the warm air, forcing it to rise. This produces a narrow band of clouds and rain.

narrow band of cloud and rain

COLD FRONT

warm air forced to rise over cold air

WARM FRONT

cold air meeting warm air

wide band of cloud and rain

ground surface

warm air

cold air

When a polar air mass with its colder, heavier air moves toward a tropical air mass with its warmer, lighter air, the cold polar air moves under the warm tropical air, forcing the warmer air to rise. As the warm air is forced up, it cools and condenses to form clouds and rain. The place where this happens is called a **cold front**.

Air masses and fronts are invisible, but they produce an endless display of weather that sweeps across the sky.

Did you know?

Because of the clouds produced along fronts, meteorologists can figure out where the fronts are. They can mark them on weather maps and satellite images.

Polar continental air masses can bring cold, dry weather like this to areas in Quebec, Canada.

What is Hazardous Weather?

Sometimes pressure, temperature, and humidity can produce very violent weather events. Unexpected weather events can have serious effects on people's lives. A severe thunderstorm is one example of a **hazardous** weather event. Other examples include violent **tornadoes** and hurricanes.

What are thunderstorms?

Thunderstorms are huge clouds accompanied by lightning, thunder, strong winds, and heavy rain. They form when warm, wet air rises and condenses to form huge, towering clouds. Thunderstorms may take from a few minutes to one hour to form.

A small cloud can develop into a huge thunderstorm in just a few minutes.

Lightning is caused by a buildup of static electricity in a thunderstorm cloud. It is like the static electricity you produce when you rub a balloon on a sweater, and then stick it to a wall. The electricity causes a giant spark (lightning) that heats the air to an incredible 54,000 °F (30,000 °C). This is five times hotter than the surface of the Sun! The rapid heating causes the air to expand explosively, which can be heard as a loud bang (thunder).

If lightning strikes close by, the thunder will be heard at the same time. If it strikes farther away you will hear the thunder a few seconds later, because light travels faster than sound. Lightning usually strikes the highest point, so it is dangerous to be on a hill or standing under a tree during a thunderstorm.

Lightning tends to strike the highest point in an area. Here it is striking the Eiffel Tower in Paris, France.

The heavy rain produced by thunderstorms may lead to **flash floods**. These happen when very heavy rain falls over a small area in a short period of time. Flash floods are very dangerous. They cause damage to homes and crops and kill over 100 people in the United States each year.

This flood in Texas was caused by extremely heavy rain during a thunderstorm in 2004.

What are tornadoes?

Tornadoes are often produced by thunderstorms, and they sometimes look like huge elephant trunks hanging down from thunder clouds. They are the most violent weather events on Earth.

A tornado is a funnel shape of spinning air. It can be 328 to 1968 feet (100 to 600 meters) across, with low pressure at the center. Wind speeds are often over 124 miles (200 kilometers) per hour and can reach 310 miles (500 kilometers) per hour. This is faster than the world's fastest trains.

Tornadoes are quite small—most are smaller than a football field —and do not last very long. Most only last for a few minutes, but they still cause an enormous amount of damage. They travel along a tornado path for about 4 miles (7 kilometers) and only cause damage in this path. A tornado might destroy all the houses on one side of a street, leaving the other side completely untouched.

Being faced with a tornado, like this one in South Dakota, can be a terrifying experience.

When the funnel touches the ground, the strong winds suck up everything in its path, including trees, animals, cars, and even people. It can carry them hundreds of feet before dropping them to the ground.

Tornadoes occur in many parts of the world, but are very common in the United States where there are over 700 tornadoes each year. They occur mainly in the "Tornado Alley", which stretches from Texas to Nebraska. They form in this region because the warm, moist air needed to form thunderstorms is found here. In May 1999 a tornado ripped through Oklahoma City, destroying thousands of homes and killing 48 people.

Did you know?

If a tornado forms above water, it is called a water spout. If a tornado forms above a desert, the funnel sucks up dust and is called a dust devil.

Tornodoes can cause huge damage, as seen in this North-Central Kentucky subdivision.

Hurricanes

Hurricanes are similar to tornadoes, but they are much bigger and they form over the sea. They often travel thousands of miles before they hit land.

Hurricanes are large low pressure systems of spiraling air, with huge clouds, strong winds, and heavy rain. They are usually around 404 miles (650 kilometers) wide. The wind speeds are often more than 99 miles (160 kilometers) per hour and can reach 186 miles (300 kilometers) per hour sometimes. The wind produces huge waves, up to 33 feet (10 meters) high that can completely swallow a ship.

Hurricanes form over warm seas close to the Equator. They are easy to recognize on satellite images because the clouds are grouped in a spiral. The center of the spiral—called the eye—is cloud-free. It is not easy, however, to predict where a hurricane will go. A hurricane heading directly for land may suddenly turn away and continue its journey across the ocean.

From above hurricanes look like giant whirlpools of clouds.

Hurricanes last for many days, but when they hit land they quickly die down as they lose energy. But before this they can cause a large amount of damage. This is because of high winds and huge waves, called **storm surges**, as well as the heavy rain that produces flooding.

Hurricanes often occur in the Caribbean, Central America, and the southeast United States. In September 2004 Hurricane Ivan struck the small island of Grenada, killing 34 people and damaging most of the houses on the island. A prison was also destroyed, and many of the prisoners escaped. The hurricane then continued through the Caribbean. Its 124-miles-per-hour (200-kilometers-per-hour) winds caused destruction in many of the islands and killed 70 people. Ivan then hit the southeast coast of the United States, causing heavy rainfall and flooding. Many roads, bridges, and buildings were damaged and 52 people were killed.

Did you know?

A hurricane along the east coast of China is called a typhoon and along the north coast of Australia it is called a Willy Willy.

This is just one building destroyed by Hurricane Ivan in 2004.

What is El Niño?

El Niño is an event that affects the weather in many parts of the world.

Winds blowing across Earth create **ocean currents**. In the Pacific Ocean there is usually a cold current in the east and a warm current in the west. The cold current is called the Peru Current, and it flows north along the west coast of South America. The cold current contains many **nutrients**, and provides food for lots of fish.

In December every year, a warm current replaces the cold Peru Current for a few weeks. This is called El Niño. The warm water contains few nutrients, so fishing is poor at this time of year.

During an El Niño event, unusually warm water along the coast of Peru causes devastating weather events in other parts of the world.

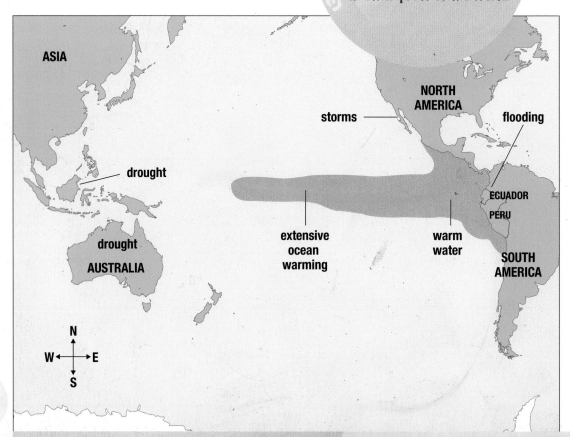

ASIA

NORTH AMERICA

storms

flooding

drought

ECUADOR

PERU

extensive ocean warming

warm water

drought

AUSTRALIA

SOUTH AMERICA

N
W E
S

Every three to seven years, El Niño conditions last for months rather than weeks. When this happens the normal situation in the Pacific Ocean is reversed. The water in the east becomes warm, and the water in the west becomes cold. The warmer water off the coast of Peru causes extreme weather conditions in different parts of the world. Nobody knows why this happens. A very severe (long lasting) El Niño in 1997–1998 caused the worst flooding Peru had ever seen. It also caused **drought** in Indonesia, southern Africa, and Australia. A drought happens when there is not enough rain. It is very serious because without rain, many crops are ruined, and less food is produced for people and animals to eat.

Did you know?

El Niño means "boy child" in Spanish. It is called this because the birth of Jesus is celebrated at Christmas, the same time of year that El Niño happens.

The 1997–1998 El Niño event caused extreme flooding in Peru.

How Do Weather Forecasts Help Us?

We have all seen weather forecasts on television. We use them to help us decide what to wear and what to do. To make weather forecasts, meteorologists at over 10,000 **weather stations** throughout the world need to constantly check the weather. The difficult nature of weather means that it is not easy to predict what will happen, so weather forecasters can sometimes get it wrong.

Weather forecasts can also be used to give warnings about hazardous weather conditions. These warnings allow people to be prepared, and many lives and homes may be saved. With the help of ship reports, aircraft reports, and satellite images, the movements and strength of hurricanes, thunderstorms, and tornadoes can be carefully watched.

Meteorologists use computers to help them predict the weather.

If it looks like one of these hazardous weather systems will strike an area, a severe weather warning is issued. A hurricane warning is given when a hurricane is within 24 hours of reaching an area. This gives people time to evacuate (leave the area). A tornado warning is given when a tornado is spotted. This usually gives people only a few minutes to take shelter, but it might be enough to save their lives.

Unfortunately weather forecasting is very difficult! The forecasts and warnings can be wrong, which can lead to people being evacuated from an area for no reason. As our understanding of these weather events increases, improved forecasts should become available to more people.

This area of North Carolina has been evacuated following a warning about Hurricane Ivan in September 2004.

Conclusion

The weather is what is happening in the atmosphere around us, in one place at one point in time. It is always changing, in some areas very quickly, in other areas very slowly. Changes in the weather are caused by changes in the air pressure, temperature, and humidity of the air as it moves from place to place.

If air remains over one place for a long period of time, an air mass will form. Where one air mass meets another, a front will form. Both air masses and fronts are invisible, but they produce an endless display of weather.

Sometimes the conditions of pressure, temperature, and humidity in the atmosphere result in very violent weather events, such as thunderstorms, tornadoes, and hurricanes. These unexpected extreme events can cause much destruction and loss of life.

The difficult nature of weather means that weather forecasters find it hard to predict what will happen. It is important to improve our understanding of the weather, because if severe weather warnings can be issued in time, many lives may be saved.

The atmosphere is about 400 miles (640 km) thick and completely encircles Earth.

Fact File

Scale	Wind speed	Description	Effects
0	37–75 mph (60–120 km/hr)	Weak	Tree branches broken, signs damaged
1	76–112 mph (121–180 km/hr)	Weak	Trees snapped in half, windows broken
2	113–156 mph (181–250 km/hr)	Strong	Large trees uprooted, mobile homes destroyed
3	157–206 mph (251–330 km/hr)	Strong	Trees blown down, cars overturned, walls removed from buildings
4	207–263 mphr (331–420 km/hr)	Violent	Buildings destroyed
5	264–313 mph (421–500 km/hr)	Violent	Cars and buildings moved over 328 feet (100 meters), large metal structures damaged

Scale	Wind speed	Description	Effects
1	75–94 mph (120–150 km/hr)	Weak	Damage to trees
2	95–106 mph (151–170 km/hr)	Moderate	Some trees blown down Some damage to roofs of buildings
3	107–125 mph (171–200 km/hr)	Strong	Large trees blown down Mobile homes destroyed Some damage to buildings Flooding at the coast Evacuation of coastal areas
4	126–156 mph (201–250 km/hr)	Very strong	Large amount of damage to buildings Flooding up to 6 miles (10 kilometers) from the coast Evacuation of coastal areas
5	Over 250 km/hr (Over 156 mph)	Devastating	All trees blown down Buildings blown down Evacuation of many areas

Glossary

air mass large body of air with similar pressure, temperature, and humidity

air pressure force of the atmosphere pushing down on Earth

anticyclone area of high pressure, also called a high

atmosphere blanket of air that surrounds Earth

barometer instrument used to measure air pressure

climate type of weather an area usually experiences

cold front front where cold polar air cuts underneath warm tropical air, forcing it to rise

condense water vapor (a gas) changing into tiny drops of liquid water

depression area of low pressure, also called a low

drought weather conditions caused when there is very little rain

El Niño warm ocean current that replaces the cold Peru current on the west coast of South America in December

energy power that is used to make something

Equator imaginary line that circles the middle of Earth

flash flood flooding that happens very quickly due to heavy rain during a thunderstorm

forecast predict what will happen in the future

front boundary between two different air masses

gravity force that keeps things on Earth

hazardous dangerous

high area of high pressure, also called an anticyclone

humidity amount of moisture in the air

hurricane very intense low pressure system of spiraling air, with huge clouds, strong winds, and heavy rain

low area of low pressure, also called a depression

meteorologist someone who studies the weather

nutrient food that plants and animals need

ocean current flow of water in an ocean caused by winds blowing the surface of the water

polar region very cold region close to the North or South Pole

precipitation rain, sleet, snow, or hail

predict say what will happen in the future

satellite image photograph taken from space

storm surge huge wave caused by a hurricane

temperature measurement of how hot or cold a place is

thermometer instrument used to measure temperature

thunderstorm storm with towering clouds, lightning, thunder, strong, gusty winds, and heavy rain

tornado funnel-shaped mass of spinning air with low pressure at the center

tropical region very hot area close to the Equator

warm front front where warm tropical air rides up over cold polar air

water vapor water in the air in the form of an invisible gas

weather condition of the atmosphere in one place at one point in time

weather stations laboratories where meteorologists record the weather

More books to read

Pipe, Jim. *Earthwise: Weather*. London: Franklin Watts, 2004.
Solway, Andrew. *A Pirate Adventure*. Chicago: Raintree, 2005.
Spilsbury, Louise and Spilsbury, Richard. *Awesome Forces of Nature:
Howling Hurricanes*. Chicago: Heinemann Library, 2004.

Index